D1458407

31

Gizmo

A Play

Alan Ayckbourn

A SAMUEL FRENCH ACTING EDITION

SAMUEL
FRENCH
FOUNDED 1830

SAMUELFRENCH.COM
SAMUELFRENCH-LONDON.CO.UK

Copyright © 1999 by Alan Ayckbourn
© 2000, Acting Edition, by Haydonning Ltd
All Rights Reserved

GIZMO is fully protected under the copyright laws of the United States
of America, the British Commonwealth, including Canada, and all other
countries of the Copyright Union. All rights, including professional and
amateur stage productions, recitation, lecturing, public reading, motion
picture, radio broadcasting, television and the rights of translation into
foreign languages are strictly reserved.

ISBN 978-0-573-15206-1

www.SamuelFrench.com
www.SamuelFrench-London.co.uk

FOR PRODUCTION ENQUIRIES

UNITED STATES AND CANADA
Info@SamuelFrench.com
1-866-598-8449

UNITED KINGDOM AND EUROPE
Plays@SamuelFrench-London.co.uk
020-7255-4302/01

Each title is subject to availability from Samuel French, depending
upon country of performance. Please be aware that GIZMO may not be
licensed by Samuel French in your territory. Professional and amateur
producers should contact the nearest Samuel French office or licensing
partner to verify availability.

CAUTION: Professional and amateur producers are hereby warned that
GIZMO is subject to a licensing fee. Publication of this play does not imply
availability for performance. Both amateurs and professionals considering a production are strongly advised to apply to the appropriate agent
before starting rehearsals, advertising, or booking a theatre. A licensing
fee must be paid whether the title is presented for charity or gain and
whether or not admission is charged.

The professional rights in this play are controlled by Casarotto Ramsay
and Associates Ltd, www.casarotto.co.uk. No one shall make any changes
in this title for the purpose of production. No part of this book may be
reproduced, stored in a retrieval system, or transmitted in any form, by
any means, now known or yet to be invented, including mechanical, elec-
tronic, photocopying, recording, videotaping, or otherwise, without the
prior written permission of the publisher. No one shall upload this title,
or part of this title, to any social media websites.

CHARACTERS

Ben Mason, a barman

In the hospital:
Professor Raymond Barth, GIZMO Project Chief
    Administrator
Dr Bernice Mallow, GIZMO Project
David Best, a neurologist
Nerys Potter, a physiotherapist
Ted Wilkins, a nurse
Sir Trevor Perkins, Chief Constable

In the park:
Rust, Dazer, Fritzo, Hezza, Dart, Tiz, gang members
Manny Rice, a businessman
Rudi, Manny's bodyguard
Keith, another bodyguard

In the flat:
Cevril Teese, Manny's girlfriend
Lando, a hit man

Audience members, passers-by, etc.

Note: Gizmo has been written with a flexible cast in
mind. With doubling, it can be done with 11 actors (8m
3f). Alternatively, it can be performed by 18 speaking
actors plus an infinite number of extras.

MUSIC USE NOTE

Licensees are solely responsible for obtaining formal written permission from copyright owners to use copyrighted music in the performance of this play and are strongly cautioned to do so. If no such permission is obtained by the licensee, then the licensee must use only original music that the licensee owns and controls. Licensees are solely responsible and liable for all music clearances and shall indemnify the copyright owners of the play(s) and their licensing agent, Samuel French, against any costs, expenses, losses and liabilities arising from the use of music by licensees. Please contact the appropriate music licensing authority in your territory for the rights to any incidental music.

IMPORTANT BILLING AND CREDIT REQUIREMENTS

If you have obtained performance rights to this title, please refer to your licensing agreement for important billing and credit requirements.

SYNOPSIS OF SCENES

The sets should ideally be as simple as possible and must in any event be designed so as to keep the scenes flowing with the minimum of hold-up between them.

GIZMO

Scene 1

A large lecture theatre in a private hospital

A number of people stand around talking quietly amongst themselves. Doctors, administrators, business people

In a moment, Professor Raymond Barth enters. With him is Dr Bernice Mallow

Barth Good morning, everybody. Would you please be seated.

A general settling down

For anyone new, I'm Ray Barth. I'm currently the PCA, the Project Chief Administrator for GIZMO, here at the Chepthorne Medley Research Hospital. I know you're all busy people so I won't waste your time. May I remind you, though, those of you who haven't attended a GIZMO briefing session before, that all information given out today is highly confidential, so please, accordingly, we request you to observe all standard Class A security procedures. No notes, photographs, filming or recordings, please. Thank you. Now I'd like to introduce Dr Bernice Mallow who will be updating us on recent developments over the past six months. Bernice.

Bernice Thank you, Ray. Good morning, everyone. Thank you for taking time to share with us. First, let me say that I see, much to my alarm, the GIZMO project is about to enter its fifteenth year.

So far it has cost a little over 25 million pounds sterling and employed over 700 doctors, technicians and micro engineers. Although I have personally only been associated with the Project for a comparatively brief six years, I am extremely conscious that there is an understandable impatience for results. Not least, I feel sure, from our funders at Chepthorne Medley. I would like, once again, to take this opportunity to thank them for their patience, for their generosity and for their unshakeable faith in GIZMO. Fifteen years in pursuit of a dream, however great, is a long time to wait. Well, patience is sometimes rewarded. Today, at long last, I am delighted to announce that we do finally have something to show. Not the whole dream—not yet—but at least, ladies and gentlemen, a part of the dream. A substantial part. A major step, certainly, on the way to a complete realization of that dream. The oasis is in sight, dawn approaches, there is light at the end of the tunnel. (*She pauses somewhat dramatically*) I want you to meet, now, two remarkable and unique men. Ladies and gentlemen, may I introduce David Best and Ben Mason.

Applause

David enters, followed by Ben. Ben is pushed on in a wheelchair by Ted

Ben, if I may talk to you first, how come the wheelchair? Do you mind telling me?

Ben (*a somewhat prepared reply*) Well, Bernice, about a year ago I was unfortunate enough to be involved in an extremely violent series of events. As a result of that, I was left over ninety per cent paralysed.

Bernice Could you be more specific, Ben? Was that the result of an attack? If so, what were the extent of your injuries?

Ben There were no injuries.

Bernice None? You mean you had no physical injuries at all, Ben?

Ben None whatsoever, Bernice. Certainly not in the way you mean.

Bernice Then what did happen precisely? David, perhaps you could help to explain?

David Well, Bernice, what happened to Ben is not that uncommon. Ben was working as a cocktail barman. He was unlucky enough to witness an appalling act of violence in the bar where he worked. A customer and his girlfriend were gunned down only inches away from him. As a result of this brutal slaying, Ben experienced a form of post-traumatic shock. If you like, he literally froze with fear. The result being as you see him now.

Bernice And he's been like this for how long, David?

David Just over fourteen months.

Bernice And let me just confirm this, his paralysis is in no way the result of any physical injury?

David Ben's so-called paralysis, Bernice, his inability to move, is purely a choice that his subconscious mind has chosen to make. At the time of the attack, he was so distressed, so terrified, that his whole nervous system instinctively shut down in an attempt to disassociate itself from what it perceived as life-threatening events. It's a natural instinct. It's in all of us. And incidentally in most mammals, too.

Bernice Like a rabbit frozen in a car's headlights?

David Precisely that.

Bernice And what happens once the danger has passed? Does the effect wear off?

David Generally instantaneously. As soon as the danger has passed. Sometimes it remains for a few seconds, or even minutes or hours. But occasionally, in a case like Ben's, it becomes semi-permanent.

Bernice And is there a cure?

David Until now, the cure has been mainly patience. Physiotherapy sometimes helps a little, at least to stop the muscles from atrophying completely, but in the end, Bernice, how can you persuade a person to move, even a person wanting to move, when there is something far stronger in their mind forbidding them to move?

Bernice Presumably, David, somehow we have to persuade them to take control of their own body again?

David Absolutely. But easier said than done, Bernice.

Bernice David, obviously you're a doctor——

David I'm a neurologist, yes...

Bernice And you've been working closely with the entire GIZMO team. How does Ben's case link in with GIZMO? Can GIZMO provide a cure for Ben's condition?

David We have great hopes that it might.

Bernice Can you explain how?

David Certainly, Bernice. (*He produces something from his pocket*) With this. (*He holds something up the size of a microchip*)

Bernice And that is what? I don't know if you can all see it, it's tiny. What is it? A microchip?

David It's a form of one, yes. It's effectively a tiny microprocessor which can be surgically implanted into the brain. It is actually covered with thousands of tiny, invisible fibres which attach themselves to the neural circuits in the brain. What effectively occurs is that this tiny device assumes control of the human body. What you're looking at here, ladies and gentlemen, is one half of GIZMO itself.

Bernice And does Ben have one of those implanted?

David Currently he does.

Bernice How does it feel, Ben?

Ben I don't honestly notice it. It felt a little odd at first but I think that was just the knowledge that it was there in my head. But I have no physical sensation of it whatsoever.

Bernice So what happens, David? Can you now send signals directly to Ben's brain? To his neuromuscular system?

David Not quite as simple as that, I'm afraid, Bernice. As you explained at the start, this is GIZMO still in its very early stages. Yes, we can send signals, but they're still quite primitive. What we've managed to come up with so far is PMRS—positive movement replication synchronicity.

Bernice Let me get that right. Positive movement replication synchronicity. Hmm. Sounds complicated. How does that work?

David Allow me to demonstrate, Bernice. Here on my wrist you see what looks at first sight like a perfectly ordinary, if somewhat bulky, wrist watch. (*He holds up his arm*) However, this is one particularly smart watch. Not only does it tell the time pretty well—(*he glances at it*)—very well, in fact—it also, via a series of built-in sensors, detects the movements made by my own body which are then transmitted virtually instantaneously to the GIZMO receiver in Ben's head. As a result of his own stimulated neural system, Ben's muscles should then move in direct synchronicity with my own. In other words, his movements should precisely imitate mine.

Bernice Sounds good in theory, David. Can we give it a try?

David Why not? I'd be happy to, Bernice.

Bernice Ben?

Ben Sure.

David Before I switch on, I'd better start from the same position Ben is starting from. So I'll take a chair—(*he does so*)—and to prove there's no trickery here, folks—I intend to sit with my back to Ben so neither of us can see each other... (*he sits now, directly behind Ben*) like so. OK. You ready, Ben?

Ben Ready.

David (*touching the watch*) Switching on.

Ben's body convulses slightly. From now on both men move almost exactly together. David grips the arms of his chair; Ben involuntarily grips the arms of his wheelchair. David rises slowly from his chair; Ben does likewise

Ben (*a little uneasily*) Hey...

Bernice Ben?

David You OK, Ben?

Ben I'm OK. I'm still a little unused to standing...

David It's OK, Ben, you're going to be fine. Just do what I do.

Ben I don't have a lot of choice, David——

David starts walking

—Whey!

The two men walk a few paces. They turn together. They wave

*almost simultaneously at the onlookers. The audience applaud.
David and Ben applaud back. They bow. As the applause continues,
they turn to face each other. They walk towards each other. They
shake hands. Bernice moves forward. She shakes hands with David.
Ben's hand goes up and down in unison with their handshake,
though he is shaking empty air. Bernice turns to Ben. She takes his
hand. Ben looks towards David a little helplessly. David executes
a handshake gesture which allows Ben to do likewise with Bernice.
David leans forward while this happens and executes a mid-air kiss.
Ben copies this, landing a kiss on Bernice's nose. The men bow once
more to the crowd who are still applauding*

> *The three then leave the platform together. The assembly stop
> applauding and get up to leave, chattering animatedly amongst
> themselves*

The Lights fade

SCENE 2

The Lights come up almost immediately on Ben's hospital bedroom

Ben is lying motionless, in his track suit, on the bed

*Ted is sitting reading. He is wearing the PMRS on his wrist. It is
apparently switched off since Ben is motionless*

A silence

Ben Are you going to be much longer?
Ted (*engrossed*) What?
Ben Reading that?
Ted Why?
Ben Because I want to get up. I want to walk about.
Ted Well, go on. Walk about, I don't mind.
Ben I can't, can I? You know that. I need you.

Pause

Look, will you switch it on, please?

Ted You want to go to the toilet?

Ben No.

Ted That's the only reason I'm supposed to switch it on. To take you to the toilet.

Ben Oh, come on, Ted.

Ted Those are my instructions. Cheer up, the physio'll be here in a minute. She'll sort you out.

Ben Thanks very much. That's all I need.

In a moment, Nerys enters. She is fit, young and hearty. She also has on a track suit and wears the PMRS on her wrist

Nerys Good morning.

Ben groans

Ted Morning.

Nerys Right! Ready, are we?

Ben No.

Ted I'll leave you to it. Have a nice time.

Ted exits

Nerys All right. Cheer up, Ben. (*She lies on the floor*) Here we go, then. Switching on. Ready? (*She switches on the GIZMO on her wrist*)

Ben's body twitches as contact is made with his nervous system

Ben Ah!

Nerys Come on. It doesn't hurt.

Ben How do you know it doesn't?

Nerys (*ignoring him*) And—up we get! (*She springs lithely to her feet*)

Ben is reluctantly forced to mimic her

Ben Ow! Steady on!
Nerys (*ploughing on regardless*) And—shake it all out. (*She shakes her body loosely*)

Ben follows suit

And—shake it all out. And—shake! And shake! And now let the head roll like this. And roll—and roll—and roll. And the other way. And roll—and roll—and roll. Good! Feeling relaxed?
Ben No.
Nerys And now the shoulders. Roll the shoulders, that's it. Roll them. Good. And roll and roll. Now, gentle jogging on the spot, remember this? Gently to start with. Keep the rest of the body relaxed. That's it, relaxed!
Ben It is relaxed! I'm not doing anything.
Nerys And a little bit faster now. (*She picks up the pace slightly*) Good. Feel it hurt a little. It ought to hurt.
Ben It does hurt.
Nerys And a little bit faster now. Sprinting, sprinting flat out. Fast as we can, come on. (*She runs on the spot vigorously*)

Ben makes agonised sounds. Nerys slows down to a walk

Good! And walk a little, now. Breathing deeply, Ben. Breathe, breathe...
Ben Can we sit down?
Nerys Sure. You want to sit down, you can sit down. I'm not stopping you.
Ben Oh, come on! You know I can only sit down if you sit down.
Nerys Me? I don't want to sit down, I want to do some more exercise. You're the one who wants to sit down. And—ready—running once again, here we go.

Another burst of concerted running. Finally, Nerys slows down again

Ben (*wheezing, very out of breath*) I think I'm going to have a heart
attack.

Nerys No, you're not, you're perfectly fit. There's nothing wrong
with you at all.

Ben Then what am I doing in here if there's nothing wrong with me?

Nerys Perfectly healthy. It's all in your mind, that's all.

Ben I know it's all in my mind. That's the whole point, you stupid
woman.

Nerys (*rather viciously*) And—bending and floor touching now.
One—two, one—two... (*She goes into a vigorous floor-touching
exercise*)

Ben is again forced to follow suit

Ben (*in agony*) Ah! Ah! I'm sorry—I didn't mean that!

Nerys (*remorselessly*) ...one—two ... one and two. And one and
two! (*She continues for several seconds, then stops*) And relax!

Ben That it, then?

Nerys Certainly not. We're just warming up, Ben. And—jogging
again gently now... Here we go.

They jog

Ben Oh, God! I'm dying. I think I'm dying...

David enters. He watches them both for a second

Nerys notices him and stops

Nerys Oh, good morning, Doctor.

David No, no, carry on, please. I'll come back later.

Ben No, no, stay! Please stay, this woman's trying to kill me!

*Throughout the next, David and Nerys talk to each other as if Ben
wasn't there. Nerys continues to exercise, forcing Ben to do likewise*

David How's he doing? Any progress?

Nerys Well, he's going to be fit, anyway. Whether he likes it or not.

Ben Listen, I'm a barman, not an Olympic athlete.

David But he's not contributing anything of his own accord?

Nerys Nothing as far as I can tell.

David It's all via the GIZMO?

Nerys So far.

David Yes, that's a worry. He ought to be contributing by now.

Ben Listen, I am here, you know. You can talk to me if you want to.

David No, it's all up there somewhere. In that mind of his. We'll get there eventually. Don't worry. (*He turns to Ben*) How are you feeling, old chap?

Ben Terrible.

David Feel like moving on your own yet, do you?

Ben I can't. I keep telling you, I can't.

David Perhaps you're not trying hard enough, old chap. Come on. Have a try.

Ben I'm telling you. I cannot move.

David Just try and walk to the bed. Stand still for a second, would you, Nerys?

Nerys does so

Come on, Ben, have a nice sit down. Wouldn't you like to try that for me?

Ben (*a motionless, internal struggle as he tries*) I—I—can't!

Nerys Come on, Ben. Try. You're not trying. You can do it. Go. Go. (*She makes little encouraging arm movements, as she speaks, urging Ben towards the bed*)

Ben copies her gestures

David (*seeing Ben's movement*) Ah, look! There was something then.

Nerys No, that was me. Sorry.

David Yes, of course. Could you switch it off a minute, Nerys? Just so he can try moving on his own?

Nerys (*doubtfully*) If you're sure.

Ben (*alarmed*) No, don't switch it——

Nerys switches off the wrist controller

(*Losing control of his body*) Aaah! (*He collapses on the floor in a heap*)
David (*not very concerned*) Whoops!
Nerys There. As you see...
David Not too clever. (*He bends down to Ben, not unkindly*) You've got to be ready to help yourself, old chap. We're all here to help you, to get you better. We're all trying our best. But in the end, it's down to you, you see?
Ben (*through gritted teeth*) Shit!
David (*straightening up*) Keep at him, Nerys. Do all you can. This project is crucial. I hardly need to tell you how much is at stake here. They're getting impatient. There's a lot of time and love gone into this. And money. We badly need a result.
Nerys I'll do my best, Doctor.
David GIZMO's far too important for this one to foul it up. Far too important...

David exits

Nerys There. Did you hear that? I hope you took note. Right. Since you're down there. Floor exercises. (*She lies down on the floor*) Ready?
Ben Oh, no!

Nerys switches on the PMRS wrist controller again. Ben's body immediately readjusts itself so that it copies her own

Nerys Legs up to ninety—and ready for cycling, away we go.

She and Ben start pedalling the air furiously, Ben groaning with the effort

The Lights fade

Scene 3

The same

The Lights come up almost at once

Ben is standing looking out of the window. Ted, still wearing the PMRS wrist-watch, stands watching him, rather bored. Ted shifts and scratches his chest. Ben is forced to do likewise. A pause. Ted scratches his head

Ben Don't do that.
Ted Sorry.

Pause

Ted sniffs and involuntarily wipes his nose with the back of his hand

Ben Look, will you stop it?
Ted All right.
Ben I don't want all your disgusting habits.
Ted My nose was itching.
Ben Well, keep your hands to yourself.

Silence

Ted You want to sit down?
Ben In a minute.
Ted Only, my feet are hurting.
Ben In a minute.
Ted It's all right for you. I've been up since six o'clock. I've been up and down the wards. Emptying the bed pans. Serving breakfasts. You're lucky I'm letting you stand up at all. I'm only supposed to take you to the toilet.
Ben Yes, I know, I know. Thank you. Incidentally, next time, would you wait till I've finished, please?
Ted How do I know when you've finished? I'm not a urologist. (*He*

indicates the watch) Look, if you don't sit down soon, I'm switching this off——

Ben You'd better not. You switch that off, I'll fall over. And if I fall over and hurt myself, you're in trouble.

Ted Well, why can't you just sit down?

Ben Because I've been sitting down for fourteen months, that's why. Except when that lunatic is forcing me to exercise. Standing here is a very wonderful experience, I can tell you.

Ted Wish I could sit down for fourteen months.

Ben You can't imagine what it's like. Just being able to look out of the window again.

Ted Lovely day.

Ben Yes. The park looks beautiful.

Ted Might look beautiful. It's full of perverts and muggers.

Ben I can't see any.

Ted Well, you won't see them, will you? They'll be lurking.

Ben Who will?

Ted The muggers. In the bushes.

Ben Rubbish.

Ted Them bushes are full of muggers.

Pause

Ben I feel like going for a walk.

Ted What?

Ben Come on. Let's go for a walk.

Ted (*alarmed*) We can't do that!

Ben Why not?

Ted We can't just go out for a walk.

Ben Why not?

Ted You're a patient. You're not allowed out for walks.

Ben Why not?

Ted Because.

Ben I'm a patient, not a prisoner.

Ted You go for a walk, they'll all start wanting to go for walks, won't they? Whole hospital'll be going for walks.

Ben Of course they won't.

Ted They might.

Ben Most of them can't walk, anyway.

Ted I can't let you go for a walk. What would Dr Best say? He'd—he'd have me.

Ben You could go for a walk.

Ted Eh?

Ben If you wanted. What if you went for a walk? I'd have to go for a walk too, then, wouldn't I?

Ted Why should I go for a walk?

Ben Better than standing here. Come on. You must be due for a break. You have one every three minutes. It's a lovely day. No one'll know. Tell you what, you walk ahead of me. Then if we're caught, you can say you didn't know I was following you.

Ted (*dubiously*) Don't know about that. Can I stop and have a fag?

Ben 'Course you can.

Ted (*considering*) I'll go first, right?

Ben You'll have to.

Ted You follow on.

Ben I've precious little choice...

Ted starts to leave cautiously. Copying him, Ben follows

Ted And don't get lost.

Ben Not unless you do.

Ted and Ben leave

Almost immediately, the Lights change

SCENE 4

The park

Occasional passers-by, etc.

Ted enters, followed at a distance by Ben

Ted (*stopping*) Just a minute.

Ben (*doing likewise*) What's the matter?

Ted Going to have my cigarette.

Ben Well, don't be too long.

Ted As long as it takes, mate. That was the deal. I'm on a break. (*He gets a cigarette out and lights it*)

Ben echoes his movements. Ted inhales gratefully. Ben does likewise

Want one?

Ben I don't smoke.

Pause. Ted smokes. Ben mimes

Ted You do now. (*He drags*) What happened, then?

Ben When?

Ted To you? What happened? How did you get like that, then?

Ben I was—I was working in this bar.

Ted Ah.

Ben There was this—young couple. Very flash, you know. Lots of jewellery. Good clothes.

Ted I know the sort.

Ben It was early on. They were the only ones in there. Both sitting at the bar. He was showing off a bit. Obviously just met her. Wanting to make an impression. Lot of drinks. Champagne cocktails, vodka stingers. She could hardly stay on her stool. Laughing away, they were.

Ted Had it coming.

Ben (*angrily*) What do you mean, had it coming? Nobody has it coming. Not like that, anyway.

Ted Some do.

Ben Anyway. They're sitting there laughing and suddenly this feller's in the doorway. I didn't even see him come in. I'm down the other end of the bar, you see, restocking the ginger ale. And he stands there, this bloke and he calls out, "Johnny" or "Gianni"— maybe "Gianni"—anyway, this other bloke's name——

Ted The one at the bar?

Ben Right. And the one at the bar, he goes as white as a sheet. And the one in the doorway says it again, "Hey, Gianni. Welcome home, Gianni". And then he brings out this gun from under his coat and he shoots him, calmly as that. In his chest.

Ted What sort of gun?

Ben I don't know. I don't know anything about guns.

Ted Machine gun?

Ben No. A pistol.

Ted Oh.

Ben One that went bang, anyway. Right in the chest. And this bloke's coughing and there's blood everywhere and the girl's screaming and holding on to him. I don't know why she didn't get out of the way, I don't know why she had to hold on to him. Why did she have to hang on to him? And this bloke starts shooting again—and naturally he hits her as well, though I don't think he meant to particularly—though maybe he did—and all of a sudden they're both of them lying there. And he's dead and she's—she's making this terrible sort of whining. Like a dog—like when my dog broke its leg... And I know she's dying as well.

Ted And then? Then what happened?

Ben This bloke with the gun, he sort of looks down at them. And he smiles. It was the most frightening smile I've ever seen in my life. And then he turns and he looks straight at me. And he's still smiling. And he says, "OK, barman," he says, "drinks on the house, eh?" And he starts walking towards me and I know then he's going to kill me, too. I know he is. Because I'd seen it all happen, you see. And I'm frozen, just frozen. Like the rabbit.

Ted (*spellbound*) Why didn't he, then? Shoot you?

Ben Someone came in from the street. They'd heard the shots and the screaming.

Ted What happened to the bloke?

Ben He dived round the counter and got out through the back.

Ted Lucky escape. For you, I mean.

Ben All that blood. I've never seen so much blood.

Ted He could've killed you.

Ben I know.

Ted He might still, I suppose. If he finds you. Would you recognize him?

Ben Mmmm?

Ted The bloke with the gun. Would you recognize him again?

Ben I'm hardly likely to forget him, am I?

Ted He could be hiding in these bushes.

Ben Great.

Ted Well. You never know. We'd better go back.

Ben If you like.

Ted You didn't tell me you was a marked man. I'd never have come out with you if I'd known you was a marked man. (*He grinds out his cigarette*)

Ben mimes the same

Looks like it's clouding over, anyway.

They start to walk again, Ben following, as before

Ted has gone only a few paces before his way is barred by Hezza, Tiz and Dart, three female gang members

Hezza Excuse me, mister, you got the price of a cup of tea?

Ted (*backing off*) No, sorry I haven't, no.

Dart Oh, come on, mister...

Tiz Mister...

Ted I got no money, get out of me way...

Hezza		Mister... Come on, mister...
Tiz	(*together*)	Mister ... give her some money...
Dart		Go on, don't be so mean, mister...

The three girls close in, cajoling him

Ted (*nervously*) Look, get out of my way, do you hear? You're not getting no money, not from me. Now piss off, all of you...

Three boys, Rust, Dazer and Fritzo appear. The girls stop their chanting. Rust is clearly their leader

Rust (*politely*) Pardon me. Are you giving these young ladies aggravation?

Ted What?

Rust Have you been frightening them?

Ted 'Course I haven't.

Rust Has he been frightening you, girls?

Dart Yes, he has.

Ted I have not.

Hezza Look at Tiz, she's shaking.

Tiz I'm shaking, look.

Rust That's appalling. What's he been doing then, girls? Exposing himself?

Ted (*indignantly*) I have not.

Dart Yeah, he was flashing at us, wasn't he, Hezz?

Hezza I was terrified. Never seen anything like it...

Ted What you talking about? I've done nothing...

Rust You disgusting old pervert...

Dazer You filth...

Fritzo You ought to be ashamed of yourself...

Rust ...corrupting innocent young girls...

Ted Innocent? What, this lot? Don't make me laugh.

Hezza Oh, thanks very much, I'm sure.

Rust Hey, hey! What are you saying? Are you suggesting these girls are not pure...?

Ted You're joking.

Rust (*indicating Hezza*) That happens to be my fiancée you're talking to.

Ted Ah, well. I didn't know that. Beg your pardon, mate...

Rust You want to be more careful. Going around flashing at other people's fiancées...

Ted Bollocks. Who're the other two, then?

Dart We're her bridesmaids.

Ted Oh, give over. Go on, get out of me way. (*He tries to push past Dart*)

Dart (*over-reacting*) Ow!
Fritzo Did you jostle her, then?
Dart He jostled me.
Tiz All right, Dart?
Fritzo First he's flashing, now he's jostling...
Dazer What's he done to you, Dart?
Dart I think he's broke my arm.
Ted I did not. How could I?
Dazer Right you, I'm having you. That's *my* fiancée whose arm you just broke.
Ted I never broke her arm. What you talking about? Let go of me...
Ben (*in alarm*) Ted!

Ted is surrounded and swamped by the gang. We lose sight of him in the mêlée. We have a clear idea of what's happening to him because, from a distance, Ben copies Ted's fate. He falls to the ground under an unseen hail of blows. He curls up to protect himself and after a few violent convulsions, lies still. The gang step back to reveal Ted in an identical position

Rust (*as they do this*) That's enough! Stand back. What's he carrying, Dart?

Dart starts to search Ted

Tiz We all going to get a share this time?
Rust No. (*To Dart*) What you got?
Dart Ten quid.
Dazer That all?
Rust Give it here.
Dart (*finding some more*) No. Wait. Eleven. Here. (*She hands the money to Rust and continues searching Ted's body*)

Rust pockets the money

Tiz Why don't we get a share?
Rust I need it.

Tiz What for?

Rust Overheads.

Tiz (*puzzled*) Overheads?

Dart Hey, Rust, look at this! (*Pleased with herself, she holds up the PMRS controller*) What about that then?

Fritzo Hey! Hey!

Hezza Look at that!

Dazer What is it?

Dart It's a wrist-watch, genius.

Hezza Big wrist-watch.

Dart It's heavy.

Rust Give it here, then.

Tiz You keeping that as well?

Rust Yes.

Tiz Overheads?

Rust No.

Tiz Why, then?

Rust Because I like it.

Fritzo, meanwhile, has discovered Ben and moves over to him

Fritzo Oy, Rust! There's another one over here.

The others turn, somewhat surprised

  Look.

Rust Did you do that?

Fritzo I never touched him.

Rust How'd he get like that?

Fritzo I dunno. He was just lying here.

Ben Hallo.

The others move over

Rust What you doing there?

Ben Just—having a lie down… (*To the others*) Hallo. Afternoon.

Dart He's a loony——

Dazer He's a dosser.

Dart (*to Rust*) Shall I search him?

Rust Might as well. (*He starts putting on the watch*) Don't mind her searching you, do you, mister?

Ben No, go ahead. (*He sees what Rust is doing*) Look, please don't play with that watch, it's a——

Ben springs abruptly to his feet as Rust puts on the watch. Dart, who was about to search Ben, springs back, somewhat startled

Dart Hey!

Rust What you playing at?

Ben Excuse me, that watch. Could you give it to me, please?

Rust What?

Ben I need that watch. I must have that watch.

Dazer Cheeky!

Rust My watch? You want my watch?

Ben No, it's my watch.

Hezza It's not your watch. It's his watch.

Dazer That nice man over there give it him.

Ben No, you don't understand...

Dart For his birthday.

Ben ...I must have that watch...

Fritzo Shall I hit him?

Rust Search him first.

Dart Right.

Dart frisks Ben somewhat expertly

Ben (*as she does this*) Look, that watch is worth practically nothing to you, I promise. But it's vital to me. It's—it monitors my medical condition, you see... That man there was a nurse...

Dart finishes her search

Rust Anything?

Dart Nothing. No ID. Nothing.

Rust Listen, you. (*He indicates Fritzo*) I ought to get him to hit you.
But I'm in a good mood. It's a sunny day, I've got a nice new
watch. Take advantage. I'm walking away now. I suggest you do
the same, eh?
Ben You don't understand...
Rust Bye, bye. (*He turns away*)

*The rest of the gang start to follow him. Ben, copying Rust, turns
away and starts to walk off in the opposite direction*

Dazer (*as Ben goes*) That's a good lad.
Ben (*still walking away*) If you'd only listen to me...

Rust stops and takes a look back over his shoulder. So does Ben

Rust Go on, then. I said, get going. (*He waits*)

So does Ben

Off you go. I won't tell you again.
Ben Look, that wrist-watch you're wearing, it's not really a watch,
it's a——
Rust (*turning to face Ben*) Hey!

Ben turns to face Rust

Do you hear me? Go! (*He points at Ben*) You—you're really
asking for it.

Ben is pointing back at Rust

Right. (*He starts to move menacingly towards Ben*)

Ben starts to move menacingly towards Rust

That's it. You've had your chance. That's it.

Hezza Get him, Rust.
Dazer Go for him, Rust.
Ben (*as he moves forward*) Listen, you must understand, this is not really me doing this. It's you doing this.

The two stop close, facing each other

Rust Yes, that's right. It's me doing this. (*He produces a knife*) It's me doing this, as well.

Ben copies Rust's action. The only difference is, he has no knife. The two start to circle each other, crouching slightly. The others gather round to watch

(*Slightly puzzled*) This is a knife, you know.
Ben (*alarmed*) I know it is. Please.

Rust feints. Ben does likewise. Rust steps back, still mystified. So does Ben

Fritzo Kill him, Rust.
Dart Go for him, Rust.
Hezza He's mad. He hasn't even got a knife.
Tiz You're gonna get killed, mister.
Rust (*springing forward*) Come on!
Ben (*springing forward*) No!

Rust, startled by Ben's leap forward, leaps back. So does Ben. He has ended up close to Tiz

Tiz (*producing a second knife; to Ben*) Here! Take this. (*She places it into his hand*)
Ben (*alarmed*) I don't want this.
Hezza What you doing, Tiz?
Tiz Even things up a bit.
Rust (*to Tiz*) I'll deal with you later.

The fight starts in earnest, though very little comes of it. The faster, more physically aggressive Rust gets, the more Ben does

(*During this*) Ha! Yeah! Come on!

These noises, one suspects, are to cover up his own increasing insecurity rather than to unsettle his opponent

Ben (*despite his aggressive actions*) Sorry ... no, I didn't mean that ... sorry, really...

As the fight continues, Manny Rice appears. He is a well-groomed, well-dressed thug, the Mr Big of the neighbourhood. He is accompanied by his regular bodyguards, Rudi and Keith

They watch for a second. Manny says something softly to Rudi

Rudi (*yelling in a terrible voice*) Oy!

The fight stops

Rust Shit!
Hezza It's Manny Rice.
Rudi Here! Come here.
Rust Me?
Rudi Yes, you. Here. Mr Rice wants a word with you.
Rust (*hastily handing his knife to Hezza*) Get rid of that.

Ben copies this by giving his knife to Tiz. Rust moves towards Manny. Ben comes with him, a few paces behind

You wanted me, Mr Rice.
Manny What's your name, boy? I know you, don't I? Rusty, isn't it? Something like that?
Rust My name's Rust, Mr Rice.
Manny Well, Rusty, you listen to me, because I'm not telling you

again. This park belongs to me. It comes within my turf. It falls within my personal remit. You understand that, do you, boy?

Rust Yes, Mr Rice.

Manny This is a peaceful park, Rusty, intended for peace-loving law-abiding people. For babies and their nannies in search of fresh air; for old age pensioners on a quest for peace and quiet; for poets and nature lovers; dog walkers and bird fanciers; pigeon feeders and squirrel strokers. You get me?

Rust Yes, Mr Rice.

Manny It is not intended for squalid little pus-ridden scumbags like you, Rusty. I will not have innocent people molested in my park, all right?

Rust We haven't been molesting.

Manny (*indicating Ted*) Then what's that gentleman doing lying on the ground there? Taking a nap?

Rust No—he had cramp. He was jogging and then he fell over. We rushed over to help him.

Manny Only in your rush your boot landed on his head.

Rust No…

Manny And I daresay you decided to loosen his clothing by relieving him of his wallet, didn't you?

Rust No…

Manny Search him, Keith.

Keith steps forward and starts to frisk Rust

Rust What you doing?

Rudi (*to the rest of the gang*) Clear off you lot, you hear? Out the park.

The gang disperses and goes off

Meanwhile, Keith kicks Rust's legs apart and forces his arms above his head. Ben follows suit

Manny (*startled at seeing this*) Who's that, then?

Rust I dunno.
Manny What's he doing?
Rust I dunno.
Manny What you doing?
Ben Sorry?
Manny Are you with him?
Ben No, I was just taking a stroll. That's my friend who was ... who fell over. (*He continues to copy Rust's contortions*)
Manny Something the matter with you?
Ben No, just taking some exercise. The point is, you see——
Manny (*to Rust*) Have your lot been troubling him as well?
Rust No.
Keith Let's have the watch, Rust.
Rust The what?
Keith You heard. Give us the watch.
Rust That's mine.
Keith (*threateningly*) Give it...
Ben No, that's what I wanted to talk to you about. That watch is actually a very sophisticated piece of equip——

At that moment, Rust removes the watch and hands it to Keith. Ben instantly collapses like a rag doll

Manny What happened? Rudi, have a look at him.

Rudi steps forward and looks at Ben

    What's the matter with him?
Rudi I don't know, Mr Rice. Could be delayed concussion.
Ben No, I'm fine really. If you'd only just give me the——
Manny Don't try and talk. Keith, get him in the car.
Keith Right. (*He is still holding the watch*) You want this, Mr Rice?
Manny Yes, give it here. (*He takes the watch from Keith and stuffs it into his pocket*)

Keith heaves Ben over his shoulder

Ben (*as this happens*) Listen, all you need to do is to take that——
Manny Don't talk! Careful with him, Keith, careful.
Keith Sorry, Mr Rice.

Keith goes off with Ben

Manny Rudi.
Rudi Mr Rice?
Manny See that one over there gets to a doctor.
Rudi Yes, Mr Rice.
Manny We can't have my park getting a bad name, can we?

*Rudi moves to Ted and during the next lifts him up in similar
fashion and carts him off in the opposite direction*

(*To Rust*) As for you, you are an aberration, boy. You know what
that means?
Rust No, Mr Rice.
Manny It means you are human ballast, son. Mislaid luggage.
Redundant footage. You are not wanted on life's voyage, all
right?
Rust Yes, Mr Rice.
Manny So take your sordid little gang of genetic deviants and
bugger off.
Rust Yes, Mr Rice.
Manny If I see you here again, come closing time they will discover
your head impaled on the spikes of the main gates, is that clear?
Rust Yes, Mr Rice.

Rust hurries off, relieved that the interview is over

Manny (*to himself*) I don't know. What's the world coming to? I
ask you. (*He calls as he goes*) Keith! Start the car.

Manny goes off. As he does so the Lights rapidly cross-fade to:

Scene 5

Manny's apartment. A bar. Two doors

Cevril, an attractive young woman in a low-cut dress, is sitting on the sofa, reading a magazine

Manny enters, followed immediately by Keith, who is still carrying Ben

Manny (*to Cevril*) Come on, shift yourself!
Cevril (*sulkily*) Why?
Manny Because we need the sofa, that's why. Put him down here, Keith.

Keith puts Ben down on the sofa, narrowly missing Cevril as she springs up

Cevril Careful!
Manny (*ignoring her, to Ben*) How you feeling?
Ben I'm perfectly fine. If you'd only let me explain...
Manny If you don't mind me saying so, son, you don't look fine to me. You can rest here. I feel responsible. Cevril will look after you.
Cevril I will?
Manny Yes, you will. All right, Keith, that'll do for now. I'll be down again in a minute.
Keith Yes, Mr Rice.

Keith goes out, under the next

Manny Now listen—what's your name again?
Ben Ben. You see, the point is——
Manny Listen, Ben, I want you to relax. Treat this place as your own. Take time to recover. I'm a hard man, Ben, but I'm a fair one—know what I mean? Person gets hurt on my turf, walking in my park through no fault of his own, then I owe him, you see.

Ben I didn't know it was your park, I thought it was St James's Park.
Manny I'm looking after it for him while he's away. No, seriously,
Ben. There's owners and then there's the real owners. There's
people who think they own things and then the people who really
own them. Know what I mean? Little lesson in life. I'll be back
in a minute. Got a little business to do, then we'll have a drink
together. Cevril, look after him. Give him anything he wants—
within reason, eh? (*He smiles*)
Cevril Looks as if he's past most things.
Manny You do as you're told.
Cevril Yes, Manny.
Manny Don't want to make Daddy cross, do you?
Cevril No, Manny.
Manny Good girl. (*He kisses her*) Here. (*He takes the watch out of
his pocket*) Look. Present for you.
Cevril What is it?
Manny What's it look like? It's a watch.
Cevril Lovely. Might as well strap Big Ben on my wrist.
Manny See you in a minute. Oh, I'm expecting Lando round here
shortly.
Cevril Oh, no...
Manny Yes! If he arrives before I'm back, offer him a drink and all.
Cevril Cyanide.
Manny Don't know what you've got against Lando, I'm sure. (*He
makes for the exit*)
Cevril Nothing at all. He's just a mad murdering psychopath but
apart from that he's perfectly charming.

Manny has gone

*Cevril turns her attention to Ben. She studies him disinterestedly.
She tosses the watch from hand to hand. Ben looks at her rather
apprehensively*

What happened to you, then? Been in a fight?
Ben It's—rather a long story.
Cevril (*shrugging*) I've got nothing else to do.

Ben I witnessed a fight. Or rather I witnessed a killing. Two killings.
Cevril (*not over-impressed*) I see.
Ben I—I was left paralysed.
Cevril What? A bullet, was it?
Ben No. Just in my mind. Do you understand?

Cevril studies him

Cevril Yes, that can happen. My sister run over a rabbit once. She can't drive at all now. Hardly get her into a car.
Ben Yes. That sort of thing.
Cevril So where did he find you, then? Manny? I thought he said in the park. What happened, you fall out your pushchair?
Ben You're not going to believe this…
Cevril Yes, I've heard that one a lot of times, go on.
Ben That watch … the one in your hand…
Cevril What about it?
Ben It's not just a watch, it's a—sort of remote controller.
Cevril (*examining it*) This?
Ben It's called a positive movement replication synchroniser…
Cevril (*unimpressed*) There now.
Ben PMRS for short.
Cevril That's handy.
Ben No, really.
Cevril Really? What you do then? You time travel with it, do you?
Ben Of course not, it——
Cevril (*speaking into the watch*) Beam me up, I am trapped here with a lunatic.
Ben Look, just put it on. Put it on and I'll show you.

Cevril stares at him suspiciously. Finally she puts on the PMRS. Nothing happens

Cevril Now what?
Ben I don't know. I've never worn it——
Cevril Oh, look! Venus! How did we get here?
Ben It's not for me, you see. It's usually worn by someone else.

Cevril It is 1746 and I am Queen Victoria.
Ben It may be switched off. Has it got a switch on it or something?
Cevril No. Only this... (*She touches something on the watch*)

Ben springs up off the couch and stands, mimicking her stance

(*Startled*) Hey——
Ben That's it!
Cevril What is?
Ben Through that you can now control my movements. As you move, I move.
Cevril (*disbelieving*) What?
Ben Try it.
Cevril Get off!
Ben Try it!

Cevril moves her arm suddenly. Ben does the same

There you are.
Cevril What are you talking about? Anyone can do that.
Ben Try it some more.

Cevril tries one or two more movements, which Ben copies

You see!
Cevril Well, you're good, I'll give you that.
Ben You believe me, then?
Cevril 'Course I don't. I'm not an idiot. I wasn't born yesterday dinner time. It's a trick, that's all.
Ben A trick?
Cevril 'Course it is.
Ben What would be the point of it?
Cevril I don't know.
Ben Well, then.
Cevril Good line in chat though, isn't it? I'm afraid when you have to go to bed, I have to go to bed as well...
Ben Oh, really...

Cevril When you have to go to the——
Ben Oh, come on! Really!
Cevril Well. (*She starts to move away*)

Ben does likewise

   Stop it.
Ben What?
Cevril Copying me. Stop it!
Ben I can't help it.
Cevril 'Course you can. Someone at school did that to me once.
Ben Really?
Cevril Kept copying me. All day. I punched her head in. (*She moves again*)

So does he

   (*Half-convinced*) I can't believe this.
Ben It's the truth.
Cevril I need a drink. (*She moves behind the bar*)

Ben follows her

   You going to follow me everywhere?
Ben Until you switch it off.
Cevril What happens when I do that?
Ben I'll fall over again.
Cevril You want one?
Ben I don't drink.
Cevril The rate you fall over you can't afford to risk it. Now, what
   shall I have? I never know what to have. (*She ponders*)
Ben May I suggest something?
Cevril You?
Ben If I may… Do you drink gin?
Cevril I drink anything.
Ben All right, then. Cocktail shaker…

Cevril I thought you didn't drink. (*She proffers it to him*) Cocktail shaker.

Ben (*hesitating, unable to take it from her*) No, hang on. It's easier for you to do it. I'll tell you what to do, OK? Put in some ice.

During the next, whilst telling her what to do, Ben echoes her movements as she obeys him

Cevril Ice. (*She puts some in the shaker*) That enough?

Ben Perfect. Angostura bitters!

Cevril (*searching for them*) Er... Angostura bitters. Yes. Got them.

Ben Just two or three drops over the ice...

She shakes the bitters into the shaker

Whoaa! That'll do! Lemon juice...

Cevril Lemon juice. Say when. (*She pours*)

Ben That's enough. Cointreau.

Cevril Cointreau. I thought you didn't drink. Say when. (*She pours*)

Ben I don't. That's it. Gin.

Cevril Gin. How do you know all this? Say when. (*She pours*)

Ben Whoaa! I used to be a barman. Lid on!

Cevril Lid on! Do you treat all your customers like this?

Ben Only the special ones... And shake.

Cevril shakes the cocktail

Cevril Say when.

Ben Keep going. A bit harder. What did you say your name was?

Cevril Cevril.

Ben What S—E—V?

Cevril No. C—E—V—R—I—L. That enough?

Ben Little bit longer. Unusual name.

Cevril Yes. The story goes that my father turned up at my christening pissed as usual and when the vicar asked him whether they'd chosen a name for me, he said several.

Ben (*laughing*) That'll do.

Cevril (*stopping*) Not a word of truth in it. Whor! I'm knackered. All this for a drink. What next?

Ben You drink it.

Cevril What, out of this?

Ben Sour glass. Got a sour glass? One of those there. No, the other one. That's it. OK. Now strain it into the glass.

Cevril (*doing so*) I hope this is going to be worth it.

Ben I guarantee it.

Cevril Right. Well, cheers!

Ben Cheers!

Cevril sips the drink cautiously

Cevril (*reacting*) Blimey!

Ben No?

Cevril Fantastic. What's it called?

Ben It's called A Maiden's Prayer.

Cevril Dead right. It's the answer to everything.

Quite suddenly, Lando enters. He stares at them

Lando Good afternoon.

Ben Afternoon.

Cevril (*sourly*) Oh, hallo, Lando.

Lando What's all this?

Cevril All what?

Lando Sorry to interrupt, I'm sure.

Cevril Not as sorry as me. 'Specially when you're the interruption.

Lando (*smiling*) You'd better learn to keep that mouth of yours shut, girl. Else one day I'm going to shut it for you.

Cevril You touch me and Manny'll tear you apart. You're just an employee round here, you know, Lando. Like the rest of us. Just in case you'd forgotten. I could put in a word, easy as that.

Lando I can wait. You're cream cake, darling, that's all. Once your cream goes off, he'll bin you. Won't last for ever, girlie. I'll be waiting. Who's he?

Cevril A friend.

Lando Of yours?

Cevril Of Manny's.

Lando (*approaching Ben*) I've seen him before. Where have I seen you?

Ben (*nervously*) Nowhere, never met.

Lando Yes. Recently. It'll come to me. (*To Cevril*) Manny's out, I take it?

Cevril He's back in a minute.

Lando So am I. (*To Ben*) You, don't run away. It'll come to me. It'll come to me. We've met somewhere.

Lando goes

Ben is breathing deeply

Cevril You all right?

Ben (*faintly*) Yes.

Cevril You're not having a turn, are you?

Ben Who is that man?

Cevril His name's Lando. He—does jobs for Manny.

Ben What sort of jobs?

Cevril Things that—Manny doesn't want to get involved with. You keep away from Lando, he's seriously dangerous. I don't frighten easy, but he scares the shit out of me. Why does he think he knows you?

Ben Because we've met before.

Cevril You sure?

Ben I'd never forget him.

Cevril Where? Where'd you meet him?

Ben In a bar.

Cevril (*incredulously*) You had a drink with him?

Ben I was working there. He came in—he shot two people—he nearly shot me.

Cevril *The Blue Parrot*? That bar?

Ben Yes, how did you know?

Cevril You were the barman, of course you were...

Ben Yes, I've just said.

Cevril (*remembering*) Yes! Of course! You're Ben…?

Ben Mason. Ben Mason.

Cevril And you really recognize him? Lando?

Ben Yes. How many more times?

Cevril And could you do that in court?

Ben Yes. I suppose so. If I was asked.

Cevril Bingo!

Ben They never traced who it was. They never charged him.

Cevril Of course they didn't. They couldn't. Because Manny gave him an alibi the size of a football ground. Come on, we'd better get you out of here. Wait! I better get changed. I can't even walk properly in this thing.

Ben What's happening?

Cevril I'll be ten seconds. Don't whatever you do move from there. (*She goes to the bedroom door*)

Ben I'll try not to. (*Despite himself, he is forced to follow her*)

Cevril closes the door in his face

Ben marches up and down on the spot against the closed door. Then as Cevril, now unseen by us, starts moving about in the bedroom changing her clothes, Ben copies her offstage actions. He undoes the imaginary dress and steps out of it. He runs to an invisible chest of drawers, opens one and, taking out a bra, puts it on. He grabs a pair of invisible jeans from a chair and struggles into them. They are tight. Finally, he wriggles his feet into loafers, whilst simultaneously pulling a T-shirt over his head. He runs his fingers through his hair as he makes a brief check in an imaginary mirror. He hurries back to the door. As he gets there, it opens and Cevril is standing in the doorway, now dressed as described

Cevril What you doing?

Ben (*rather guiltily*) Waiting for you.

Cevril Well, come on then, out the way. (*She realizes he can't*) Oh. Sorry. (*She steps to one side*)

Ben does likewise. Cevril moves into the room

Ben goes into the bedroom and disappears

(*Turning*) Where are you going?

Ben (*off*) Sorry. I can't help it. We seem to have got out of sync.

Cevril Well, you can't stay in there. We need to be out of here. Come on out.

Ben (*off*) I can't. Tell you what, walk towards me a bit. If you walk this way, then that'll cause me to walk that way.

Cevril Then I'll be in the bedroom.

Ben Give it a try.

Cevril walks towards the bedroom door

As she nears it, Ben comes out

They are now facing each other

Cevril Now what do we do?

Ben You'll have to turn me round by hand. We both need to be facing the same way.

Cevril Right. (*She grabs him by the shoulders*)

He grabs her. They wrestle

(*Struggling*) No, don't you—turn me—I'm supposed to be turning you...

Ben (*also struggling*) I'm sorry, I can't—help it...

Cevril (*giving up the struggle*) This is ridiculous. (*As she regains her breath, a sudden thought*) Incidentally, when I was in there just now, were you doing what I was doing? You must have been.

Ben (*vaguely*) Only sort of.

Cevril Glad I didn't do anything else. Tell you what, I'll go round the back of you, we'll try that.

Cevril edges round the back of Ben as he edges round the back of her

Good … good… (*Now back to back with Ben, she swiftly turns to him*)

Ben immediately turns to face her

Oh, gawd! This is hopeless. Look, Ben, I'm sorry to do this to you, love, but there really isn't time. (*She switches off the PMRS*)

Ben collapses

Ben Ah!

Cevril Sorry. This is the only way, I'm afraid. If Lando comes back and recognizes you, we're both dead. (*With an effort, she grabs him under the armpits and starts to haul him towards the front door*)

As they reach it, the door opens and Manny comes in

Cevril drops Ben and steps back

Hallo, Manny.

Manny What you doing?

Cevril I was——

Manny Eh?

Cevril I was—just giving him a move round.

Manny Why are you dressed like that?

Cevril I was just——

Manny You know I don't like you dressed like that. I hate it when you dress like that. Now go in there and get changed.

Cevril No, I need to go out, Manny, I need to——

Manny (*quietly*) You're not arguing with Daddy, are you, Cevril?

Cevril No, I wasn't. I don't argue with Daddy.

Manny Because that's naughty that is. And we always agreed good behaviour, didn't we?

Cevril (*meekly*) Yes, Manny. (*She nervously fingers the PMRS*)

Manny Naughty girl. Daddy gives you everything you want,

doesn't he? Nice sports car, jewellery, lots of good clothes, two thousand bloody pairs of shoes, even that nice watch there——
Cevril Yes. (*She activates the PMRS*)

Unseen by Manny, Ben regains his feet so that he stands close behind him

Manny But all that depends, Cevril, on you doing exactly what Daddy tells you, doesn't it?
Cevril Yes, Manny. (*She swings her right arm to and fro in a gesture of apparent apology*)

Positioned behind Manny, Ben does the same

Manny Now I've had to punish you once before, remember.
Cevril Yes, Manny.
Manny I don't want to have to do that again because it hurt me more than it hurt you, believe me. Now, you get back in that bedroom and——

Cevril swings her arm and chops the air with the edge of her hand

Cevril Hah!

Ben mirrors this, only his blow connects with the back of Manny's neck. Manny goes down like a felled tree

Ben (*alarmed*) Ah! Did I do that?
Cevril No, I did.
Ben Who the hell are you?
Cevril Detective Sergeant Turner. Undercover Vice Squad. Come on, let's move it!
Ben What about him? Is he dead?
Cevril He'll be fine.
Ben More than my hand will.

Cevril kneels by Manny's body. Ben does likewise

What are you doing?
Cevril Taking his gun. Just in case we meet Lando on the stairs.
Ben Oh, my God. I'm going to have a relapse in a minute.

Cevril finds the gun

Cevril Got it! Right, off we go. (*She stands*)

Ben stands

Just check the coast is clear.
Ben Excuse me…
Cevril What?
Ben I'm still facing the wrong way.
Cevril Be with you in a minute. (*She moves cautiously to the door*)
Ben Excuse me…
Cevril (*mildly irritated*) What now?
Ben What's your real name, then? Your first name.
Cevril Cevril. It's still Cevril.
Ben (*smiling*) Oh, good. I'm glad.
Cevril (*smiling in turn*) Honestly. (*She opens the door slowly, the gun in her other hand*)

Lando is standing there

Lando (*smiling*) Back again.

Cevril steps back involuntarily and brings the gun up to point at him. But Lando is quicker. He steps into the room and chops down on her wrist. Cevril drops the gun somewhere in the middle of the room

Now, now, now…

Cevril aims a blow at him which he blocks. They are obviously evenly matched. Once again all Cevril's moves are matched by Ben, albeit somewhat ineffectually. Several more moves and then Lando has her in an arm lock

Cevril (*in pain*) Ben ... help me...

Lando No good asking your boyfriend, darling. He's not going to help you. I've met him before. He's a rabbit, a scared little rabbit...

Cevril elbows him, twists and escapes into the bedroom. Lando follows, highly amused

(*Off*) No way out that way, darling. Not unless you fancy the window.

The fight now continues offstage. We hear it and see some of it, thanks to Ben's one-sided re-enactment of Cevril's side. Cevril initially gives as good as she takes but eventually Lando apparently, judging from Ben's reaction, catches her by the throat. Ben's hand gropes behind him as he chokes. His fingers find some object which he swings up towards his assailant's head. A cry from offstage as Lando is struck. As a result of this, Cevril, according to Ben, is pushed backwards with some force. Flailing his arms, Ben tries to keep his balance. A crash of broken glass from the bedroom. A cry from Cevril

Ben (*echoing her cry*) Cevril!

We see Ben apparently in mid air for a second. He falls on his back. He lies there. Silence. From the bedroom, the sound of someone crawling with great effort along the floor

(*Calling, softly*) Cevril!

Lando appears in the doorway. His face is covered in blood from a deep cut in his head

Lando (*talking with difficulty*) Gone out the window, barman. Not good for your health from the fifth floor. 'Fraid she's passed on to that great cocktail lounge in the sky. Forget her now. We've got our own little bit of business to finish, haven't we, barman? (*He* *starts to crawl painfully across the floor towards the gun and Ben)* Here I come, Ben. On my way.

With a supreme effort, Ben sits up. It is clear that he is doing this on his own. He looks at the gun

(*Divining Ben's intention*) Come on, then. Come on, race you, Ben. Race you…

The two men crawl with difficulty towards the gun. They are finally both within reach and make a simultaneous grab for it

Black-out. A single shot

SCENE 6

The Lights swiftly come up on the hospital lecture room as in Scene 1

The audience is gathered as before. Amongst the dignitaries on the platform are Professor Barth, Dr Bernice Mallow, David Best, Nerys Potter and Sir Trevor Perkins. Barth is in mid-flow

Barth …and it is perhaps only fitting that this award ceremony should take place here at the Chepthorne Medley Research Hospital. If it were not for the outstanding work by the GIZMO team, these extraordinary strides forward in the history of medicine would never have been made. We would not be standing here today to celebrate this truly inspiring display of human bravery and courage. I would therefore like to call upon the Chief Constable, Sir Trevor Perkins, to make the presentation.

Applause. Barth sits. Perkins steps forward

Perkins Thank you. I'd just like to add that these actions have made a considerable contribution towards our constant and unceasing war against crime. Thanks to this individual gallantry, together with some remarkable back-up police work by our Rapid Response Team, we have struck a strong blow against the gangs that terrorise and presume to own our cities. I have great pleasure in giving this Fiberts Modular Plastics Award for Outstanding Bravery in the Community to Ben Mason.

Applause

Ben steps on to the stage and accepts the award. He is now moving normally under his own steam

Ben Thank you very much. Thank you. I would just like to say firstly, how much I owe to the Institute and in particular to the GIZMO project which I'm pleased to say is now becoming widely accepted as an important treatment for a wide range of post trauma and remedial work. As regards this award, well, if it belongs to anyone, it belongs to Detective Sergeant Cevril Turner who is quite simply one of the most remarkable, one of the bravest people I have ever been privileged to meet. Thank you.

Applause. Ben moves swiftly back to the side of the platform

Perkins And so to our second award, and—here I think my work's already been done for me—the second Bravery Award to Detective Sergeant—Cervil—(*aside, to Barth*)—sorry, is that…?
Barth Cevril.
Perkins Cevril—sorry—Detective Sergeant Cevril Turner.

Cevril is pushed on in a wheelchair by Ted

Applause and cheers. She is presented with her award by Perkins who then sits down

Cevril (*for once lost for words*) What can I say? Thank you. That's all. I'm very lucky to be alive, I suppose. Thanks to all these wonderful people. Thank you, everyone. Thank you, Ben. Thank you.

Applause. Barth rises, signalling for silence

Barth There is a sort of footnote to today's events which may be of interest to you. As you probably know, Sergeant Turner received spinal injuries as a result of her fall. Injuries which have left her, for several months, totally paralysed. However, thanks to GIZMO, our story does come more or less full circle—*(he looks over to Ben)*—Ben, would you mind?

Ben reveals a PMRS on his wrist. He switches it on. In her wheelchair, Cevril twitches. Ben rises slowly; so does Cevril. Applause. Ben steps forward; she does the same. They turn and walk towards each other. He holds out his hand; she does the same. They turn to face their audience and bow together. They turn back to face each other, Cevril looking slightly startled. Ben kisses her. Cevril, whether she likes it or not (and one rather gathers she does), responds

The Lights fade to Black-out

FURNITURE AND PROPERTY LIST

Further dressing may be added at the director's discretion

SCENE 1

On stage: Chair with arms

Off stage: Wheelchair for **Ben (Ted)**

Personal: **David:** microchip, PMRS wrist-watch

SCENE 2

On stage: Bed
              Book

Personal: **Ted:** PMRS wrist-watch (worn throughout)
              Nerys: PMRS wrist-watch

SCENE 3

On stage: As before

SCENE 4

Strike: Bed
              Book

Personal: **Ted:** cigarette, lighter, wallet containing 11 pounds
              Rust: knife
              Tiz: knife

SCENE 5

On stage: Bar. *In it*: cocktail shaker, ice, angostura bitters, lemon
juice, Cointreau, gin, sour glass
Sofa
Magazine

Personal: **Manny:** PMRS wrist-watch, gun

SCENE 6

On stage: Awards

Off stage: **Cevril** in wheelchair (**Ted**)

Personal: **Ben:** PMRS wrist-watch

LIGHTING PLOT

Property fittings required: nil
Various interior and exterior settings

SCENE 1

To open: Overall general lighting

Cue 1   **All** exit   (Page 6)
          Fade lights

SCENE 2

To open: Overall general lighting

Cue 2   **Nerys** and **Ben** start pedalling   (Page 11)
          Fade lights

SCENE 3

To open: Overall general lighting

Cue 3   **Ted** and **Ben** leave   (Page 14)
          Change lights for next scene

SCENE 4

To open:	Sunny outdoor lighting	
Cue 4	**Manny** exits *Cross-fade to next scene*	(Page 27)

SCENE 5

To open:	Overall indoor lighting	
Cue 5	**Ben** and **Lando** reach for gun *Black-out*	(Page 42)

SCENE 6

To open:	Overall indoor lighting	
Cue 6	**Ben** and **Cevril** kiss *Fade lights to black-out*	(Page 44)

Lightning Source UK Ltd.
Milton Keynes UK
UKOW03f0619250714

235742UK00001B/2/P